MW00449029

Order My Steps: A Guided Journal for Boys

Copyright © 2016 by My Learning Partners, LLC

Ordering Information:
Quantity sales. Special discounts are available on quantity purchases by churches, organizations, associations, and others. For information, please e-mail info@mylearningpartners.com.

Printed in the United States of America

How to Use This Journal

This guided journal was created to help you journey through life being guided by God's directions. God knows every step of your journey and He promises to be there with you along the way. By understanding Bible verses, you can discover God's promises. You can become closer to God and stay in step with Him as he shows you the way. As long as you stay close to God, you will take steps in the right direction. You will be able to use Bible verses to help you make better choices about how you treat yourself and other people.

The pages are filled with coloring sheets and guided journal pages to help you understand and memorize the Bible verses. It is important to both understand and memorize the verses so that you can recite them to remind yourself when it is time for you to make choices in life. The selected Bible verses are encouraging and thought-provoking. The coloring pages and the journal prompts are designed to be reflective. While you color the area around the bible verse, you can recite the words and think about what each word means. When answering the guided journal prompt, you will apply the bible verse to your own life and experiences.

Each journal prompt repeats the S.T.E.P. model:

S stands for Summarize. When you summarize, you will put in your own words what you believe the Bible verse means.

T stands for Think. As you think about the verse, you will write down what you think God is telling you to do.

E stands for Explain. You will explain how the Bible verse relates to your own life experience or you will give an example of how the verse can be used to deal with a real-life situation.

P stands for Prayer. You will use the Bible verse or specific words from the verse to write a prayer.

There are 52 bible verses in <u>Order My Steps</u>. This journal is designed for you to focus on one verse each week. Each verse will remind you of God's presence in your life and inspire you to be guided by God. You will teach your brain and your heart to think about making the best choices. You will get to know God and develop a relationship with Him that allows you to hear His advice when faced with difficult decisions.

FOR

FROM

DATE

TABLE OF CONTENTS

THE LORD IS MY SHEPHERD.
I HAVE EVERYTHING I NEED.
HE GIVES ME REST IN GREEN PASTURES.
HE LEADS ME TO CALM WATER.
HE GIVES ME NEW STRENGTH.
FOR THE GOOD OF HIS NAME,
HE LEADS ME ON PATHS THAT ARE RIGHT
EVEN IF I WALK
THROUGH A VERY DARK VALLEY,
I WILL NOT BE AFRAID,
BECAUSE YOU ARE WITH ME.
PSALM 23

S UMMARIZE IN YOUR OWN WORDS.
WHAT IS THIS BIBLE VERSE ABOUT?

not being fearful and
knowing God is withus

T HINK ABOUT GOD'S ADVICE AND HIS PROMISE IN THIS VERSE.
WHAT IS HE TELLING YOU TO DO?

do not be afraid

E XPLAIN HOW THIS BIBLE VERSE RELATES TO YOUR EXPERIENCES.
HOW CAN YOU USE THIS VERSE IN YOUR OWN LIFE?

When I am afraid

P PRAY FOR GOD'S GUIDANCE AND HELP. WRITE A PRAYER LETTER
TO GOD. USE WORDS OR PHRASES FROM THE BIBLE VERSE.

Dear God, Thank you
for Meow Meow and my
family

Page 2

S UMMARIZE IN YOUR OWN WORDS.
WHAT IS THIS BIBLE VERSE ABOUT?

T HINK ABOUT GOD'S ADVICE AND HIS PROMISE IN THIS VERSE.
WHAT IS HE TELLING YOU TO DO?

E XPLAIN HOW THIS BIBLE VERSE RELATES TO YOUR EXPERIENCES.
HOW CAN YOU USE THIS VERSE IN YOUR OWN LIFE?

P PRAY FOR GOD'S GUIDANCE AND HELP. WRITE A PRAYER LETTER
TO GOD. USE WORDS OR PHRASES FROM THE BIBLE VERSE.

DO NOT BE SHAPED BY THIS WORLD. INSTEAD, BE CHANGED BY A NEW WAY OF THINKING. THEN YOU WILL BE ABLE TO DECIDE WHAT GOD WANTS FOR YOU. YOU WILL BE ABLE TO KNOW WHAT IS GOOD AND PLEASING TO GOD.

ROMANS 12:2

S UMMARIZE IN YOUR OWN WORDS.
WHAT IS THIS BIBLE VERSE ABOUT?

T HINK ABOUT GOD'S ADVICE AND HIS PROMISE IN THIS VERSE.
WHAT IS HE TELLING YOU TO DO?

E XPLAIN HOW THIS BIBLE VERSE RELATES TO YOUR EXPERIENCES.
HOW CAN YOU USE THIS VERSE IN YOUR OWN LIFE?

P PRAY FOR GOD'S GUIDANCE AND HELP. WRITE A PRAYER LETTER
TO GOD. USE WORDS OR PHRASES FROM THE BIBLE VERSE.

S UMMARIZE IN YOUR OWN WORDS. WHAT IS THIS BIBLE VERSE ABOUT?

T HINK ABOUT GOD'S ADVICE AND HIS PROMISE IN THIS VERSE. WHAT IS HE TELLING YOU TO DO?

E XPLAIN HOW THIS BIBLE VERSE RELATES TO YOUR EXPERIENCES. HOW CAN YOU USE THIS VERSE IN YOUR OWN LIFE?

P PRAY FOR GOD'S GUIDANCE AND HELP. WRITE A PRAYER LETTER TO GOD. USE WORDS OR PHRASES FROM THE BIBLE VERSE.

S UMMARIZE IN YOUR OWN WORDS. WHAT IS THIS BIBLE VERSE ABOUT?

T HINK ABOUT GOD'S ADVICE AND HIS PROMISE IN THIS VERSE. WHAT IS HE TELLING YOU TO DO?

E XPLAIN HOW THIS BIBLE VERSE RELATES TO YOUR EXPERIENCES. HOW CAN YOU USE THIS VERSE IN YOUR OWN LIFE?

P PRAY FOR GOD'S GUIDANCE AND HELP. WRITE A PRAYER LETTER TO GOD. USE WORDS OR PHRASES FROM THE BIBLE VERSE.

S UMMARIZE IN YOUR OWN WORDS. WHAT IS THIS BIBLE VERSE ABOUT?

T HINK ABOUT GOD'S ADVICE AND HIS PROMISE IN THIS VERSE. WHAT IS HE TELLING YOU TO DO?

E XPLAIN HOW THIS BIBLE VERSE RELATES TO YOUR EXPERIENCES. HOW CAN YOU USE THIS VERSE IN YOUR OWN LIFE?

P PRAY FOR GOD'S GUIDANCE AND HELP. WRITE A PRAYER LETTER TO GOD. USE WORDS OR PHRASES FROM THE BIBLE VERSE.

SUMMARIZE IN YOUR OWN WORDS.
WHAT IS THIS BIBLE VERSE ABOUT?

THINK ABOUT GOD'S ADVICE AND HIS PROMISE IN THIS VERSE.
WHAT IS HE TELLING YOU TO DO?

EXPLAIN HOW THIS BIBLE VERSE RELATES TO YOUR EXPERIENCES.
HOW CAN YOU USE THIS VERSE IN YOUR OWN LIFE?

PRAY FOR GOD'S GUIDANCE AND HELP. WRITE A PRAYER LETTER
TO GOD. USE WORDS OR PHRASES FROM THE BIBLE VERSE.

DON'T JUDGE OTHER PEOPLE, AND YOU WILL NOT BE JUDGED. DON'T ACCUSE OTHERS OF BEING GUILTY, AND YOU WILL NOT BE ACCUSED OF BEING GUILTY. FORGIVE OTHER PEOPLE, AND YOU WILL BE FORGIVEN. LUKE 6:37

S UMMARIZE IN YOUR OWN WORDS.
WHAT IS THIS BIBLE VERSE ABOUT?

T HINK ABOUT GOD'S ADVICE AND HIS PROMISE IN THIS VERSE.
WHAT IS HE TELLING YOU TO DO?

E XPLAIN HOW THIS BIBLE VERSE RELATES TO YOUR EXPERIENCES.
HOW CAN YOU USE THIS VERSE IN YOUR OWN LIFE?

P PRAY FOR GOD'S GUIDANCE AND HELP. WRITE A PRAYER LETTER
TO GOD. USE WORDS OR PHRASES FROM THE BIBLE VERSE.

THE ONLY TEMPTATIONS THAT YOU HAVE
ARE THE TEMPTATIONS THAT ALL PEOPLE
HAVE. BUT YOU CAN TRUST GOD. HE WILL
NOT LET YOU BE TEMPTED MORE THAN
YOU CAN STAND. BUT WHEN YOU ARE
TEMPTED, GOD WILL ALSO GIVE YOU A
WAY TO ESCAPE THAT TEMPTATION.
THEN YOU WILL BE ABLE TO STAND IT.
1 CORINTHIANS 10:13

S UMMARIZE IN YOUR OWN WORDS.
WHAT IS THIS BIBLE VERSE ABOUT?

T HINK ABOUT GOD'S ADVICE AND HIS PROMISE IN THIS VERSE.
WHAT IS HE TELLING YOU TO DO?

E XPLAIN HOW THIS BIBLE VERSE RELATES TO YOUR EXPERIENCES.
HOW CAN YOU USE THIS VERSE IN YOUR OWN LIFE?

P PRAY FOR GOD'S GUIDANCE AND HELP. WRITE A PRAYER LETTER
TO GOD. USE WORDS OR PHRASES FROM THE BIBLE VERSE.

DEAR FRIENDS, WE SHOULD
LOVE EACH OTHER, BECAUSE
LOVE COMES FROM GOD. THE
PERSON WHO LOVES HAS
BECOME GOD'S CHILD AND
KNOWS GOD. WHOEVER
DOES NOT LOVE DOES
NOT KNOW GOD,
BECAUSE GOD IS LOVE.
1 JOHN 4:7-8

SUMMARIZE IN YOUR OWN WORDS.
WHAT IS THIS BIBLE VERSE ABOUT?

THINK ABOUT GOD'S ADVICE AND HIS PROMISE IN THIS VERSE.
WHAT IS HE TELLING YOU TO DO?

EXPLAIN HOW THIS BIBLE VERSE RELATES TO YOUR EXPERIENCES.
HOW CAN YOU USE THIS VERSE IN YOUR OWN LIFE?

PPRAY FOR GOD'S GUIDANCE AND HELP. WRITE A PRAYER LETTER
TO GOD. USE WORDS OR PHRASES FROM THE BIBLE VERSE.

JESUS SAID, "DON'T LET YOUR HEARTS BE TROUBLED. TRUST IN GOD. AND TRUST IN ME."
JOHN 14:1

S UMMARIZE IN YOUR OWN WORDS.
WHAT IS THIS BIBLE VERSE ABOUT?

T HINK ABOUT GOD'S ADVICE AND HIS PROMISE IN THIS VERSE.
WHAT IS HE TELLING YOU TO DO?

E XPLAIN HOW THIS BIBLE VERSE RELATES TO YOUR EXPERIENCES.
HOW CAN YOU USE THIS VERSE IN YOUR OWN LIFE?

P PRAY FOR GOD'S GUIDANCE AND HELP. WRITE A PRAYER LETTER
TO GOD. USE WORDS OR PHRASES FROM THE BIBLE VERSE.

THE LORD FORGIVES ME FOR ALL MY SINS. HE HEALS ALL MY DISEASES. HE SAVES MY LIFE FROM THE GRAVE. HE LOADS ME WITH LOVE AND MERCY.

PSALM 103:3-4

S UMMARIZE IN YOUR OWN WORDS.
WHAT IS THIS BIBLE VERSE ABOUT?

T HINK ABOUT GOD'S ADVICE AND HIS PROMISE IN THIS VERSE.
WHAT IS HE TELLING YOU TO DO?

E XPLAIN HOW THIS BIBLE VERSE RELATES TO YOUR EXPERIENCES.
HOW CAN YOU USE THIS VERSE IN YOUR OWN LIFE?

P PRAY FOR GOD'S GUIDANCE AND HELP. WRITE A PRAYER LETTER
TO GOD. USE WORDS OR PHRASES FROM THE BIBLE VERSE.

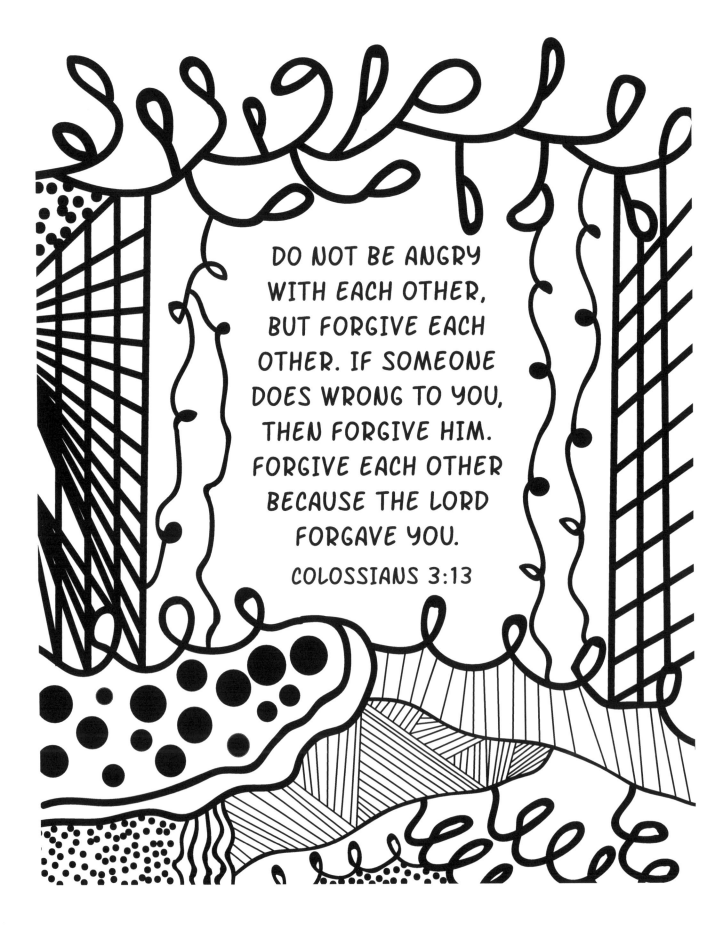

S UMMARIZE IN YOUR OWN WORDS.
WHAT IS THIS BIBLE VERSE ABOUT?

T HINK ABOUT GOD'S ADVICE AND HIS PROMISE IN THIS VERSE.
WHAT IS HE TELLING YOU TO DO?

E XPLAIN HOW THIS BIBLE VERSE RELATES TO YOUR EXPERIENCES.
HOW CAN YOU USE THIS VERSE IN YOUR OWN LIFE?

P PRAY FOR GOD'S GUIDANCE AND HELP. WRITE A PRAYER LETTER
TO GOD. USE WORDS OR PHRASES FROM THE BIBLE VERSE.

YOU CAN BE
SURE THAT I WILL BE
WITH YOU ALWAYS. I
WILL CONTINUE WITH
YOU UNTIL THE END
OF THE WORLD.

MATTHEW 28:20

S UMMARIZE IN YOUR OWN WORDS. WHAT IS THIS BIBLE VERSE ABOUT?

T HINK ABOUT GOD'S ADVICE AND HIS PROMISE IN THIS VERSE. WHAT IS HE TELLING YOU TO DO?

E XPLAIN HOW THIS BIBLE VERSE RELATES TO YOUR EXPERIENCES. HOW CAN YOU USE THIS VERSE IN YOUR OWN LIFE?

P PRAY FOR GOD'S GUIDANCE AND HELP. WRITE A PRAYER LETTER TO GOD. USE WORDS OR PHRASES FROM THE BIBLE VERSE.

A WISE PERSON IS CAREFUL AND STAYS OUT OF TROUBLE. BUT A FOOLISH PERSON IS QUICK TO ACT AND CARELESS. A PERSON WHO QUICKLY LOSES HIS TEMPER DOES FOOLISH THINGS. BUT A PERSON WITH UNDERSTANDING REMAINS CALM.
PROVERBS 14:16-17

S UMMARIZE IN YOUR OWN WORDS.
WHAT IS THIS BIBLE VERSE ABOUT?

T HINK ABOUT GOD'S ADVICE AND HIS PROMISE IN THIS VERSE.
WHAT IS HE TELLING YOU TO DO?

E XPLAIN HOW THIS BIBLE VERSE RELATES TO YOUR EXPERIENCES.
HOW CAN YOU USE THIS VERSE IN YOUR OWN LIFE?

P PRAY FOR GOD'S GUIDANCE AND HELP. WRITE A PRAYER LETTER
TO GOD. USE WORDS OR PHRASES FROM THE BIBLE VERSE.

I WILL NOT BE AFRAID
BECAUSE THE LORD
IS WITH ME.
PEOPLE CAN'T DO
ANYTHING TO ME.
PSALM 118:6

S UMMARIZE IN YOUR OWN WORDS.
WHAT IS THIS BIBLE VERSE ABOUT?

T HINK ABOUT GOD'S ADVICE AND HIS PROMISE IN THIS VERSE.
WHAT IS HE TELLING YOU TO DO?

E XPLAIN HOW THIS BIBLE VERSE RELATES TO YOUR EXPERIENCES.
HOW CAN YOU USE THIS VERSE IN YOUR OWN LIFE?

P PRAY FOR GOD'S GUIDANCE AND HELP. WRITE A PRAYER LETTER
TO GOD. USE WORDS OR PHRASES FROM THE BIBLE VERSE.

GOD HAS CHOSEN YOU
AND MADE YOU HIS HOLY
PEOPLE. HE LOVES YOU.
SO ALWAYS DO THESE
THINGS: SHOW MERCY
TO OTHERS; BE KIND,
HUMBLE, GENTLE,
AND PATIENT.
COLOSSIANS 3:12

S
UMMARIZE IN YOUR OWN WORDS.
WHAT IS THIS BIBLE VERSE ABOUT?

T
HINK ABOUT GOD'S ADVICE AND HIS PROMISE IN THIS VERSE.
WHAT IS HE TELLING YOU TO DO?

E
XPLAIN HOW THIS BIBLE VERSE RELATES TO YOUR EXPERIENCES.
HOW CAN YOU USE THIS VERSE IN YOUR OWN LIFE?

P
PRAY FOR GOD'S GUIDANCE AND HELP. WRITE A PRAYER LETTER
TO GOD. USE WORDS OR PHRASES FROM THE BIBLE VERSE.

BUT THE HELPER WILL TEACH YOU EVERYTHING. HE WILL CAUSE YOU TO REMEMBER ALL THE THINGS I TOLD YOU. THIS HELPER IS THE HOLY SPIRIT WHOM THE FATHER WILL SEND IN MY NAME.
JOHN 14:26

S UMMARIZE IN YOUR OWN WORDS. WHAT IS THIS BIBLE VERSE ABOUT?

T HINK ABOUT GOD'S ADVICE AND HIS PROMISE IN THIS VERSE. WHAT IS HE TELLING YOU TO DO?

E XPLAIN HOW THIS BIBLE VERSE RELATES TO YOUR EXPERIENCES. HOW CAN YOU USE THIS VERSE IN YOUR OWN LIFE?

P PRAY FOR GOD'S GUIDANCE AND HELP. WRITE A PRAYER LETTER TO GOD. USE WORDS OR PHRASES FROM THE BIBLE VERSE.

I WILL LOOK TO THE
LORD FOR HELP. I
WILL WAIT FOR GOD
TO SAVE ME. MY
GOD WILL HEAR ME.
MICAH 7:7

S UMMARIZE IN YOUR OWN WORDS. WHAT IS THIS BIBLE VERSE ABOUT?

T HINK ABOUT GOD'S ADVICE AND HIS PROMISE IN THIS VERSE. WHAT IS HE TELLING YOU TO DO?

E XPLAIN HOW THIS BIBLE VERSE RELATES TO YOUR EXPERIENCES. HOW CAN YOU USE THIS VERSE IN YOUR OWN LIFE?

P PRAY FOR GOD'S GUIDANCE AND HELP. WRITE A PRAYER LETTER TO GOD. USE WORDS OR PHRASES FROM THE BIBLE VERSE.

TWO PEOPLE ARE
BETTER THAN ONE.
THEY GET MORE DONE BY
WORKING TOGETHER. IF
ONE PERSON FALLS,
THE OTHER CAN HELP
HIM UP. BUT IT IS BAD
FOR THE PERSON WHO IS
ALONE WHEN HE FALLS.
NO ONE IS THERE TO
HELP HIM.
  ECCLESIASTES 4:9-10

S UMMARIZE IN YOUR OWN WORDS.
WHAT IS THIS BIBLE VERSE ABOUT?

T HINK ABOUT GOD'S ADVICE AND HIS PROMISE IN THIS VERSE.
WHAT IS HE TELLING YOU TO DO?

E XPLAIN HOW THIS BIBLE VERSE RELATES TO YOUR EXPERIENCES.
HOW CAN YOU USE THIS VERSE IN YOUR OWN LIFE?

P PRAY FOR GOD'S GUIDANCE AND HELP. WRITE A PRAYER LETTER
TO GOD. USE WORDS OR PHRASES FROM THE BIBLE VERSE.

DO EVERYTHING WITHOUT COMPLAINING OR ARGUING. THEN YOU WILL BE INNOCENT AND WITHOUT ANYTHING WRONG IN YOU. YOU WILL BE GOD'S CHILDREN WITHOUT FAULT. BUT YOU ARE LIVING WITH CROOKED AND MEAN PEOPLE ALL AROUND YOU. AMONG THEM YOU SHINE LIKE STARS IN THE DARK WORLD.
PHILIPPIANS 2:14-15

S UMMARIZE IN YOUR OWN WORDS.
WHAT IS THIS BIBLE VERSE ABOUT?

T HINK ABOUT GOD'S ADVICE AND HIS PROMISE IN THIS VERSE.
WHAT IS HE TELLING YOU TO DO?

E XPLAIN HOW THIS BIBLE VERSE RELATES TO YOUR EXPERIENCES.
HOW CAN YOU USE THIS VERSE IN YOUR OWN LIFE?

P PRAY FOR GOD'S GUIDANCE AND HELP. WRITE A PRAYER LETTER
TO GOD. USE WORDS OR PHRASES FROM THE BIBLE VERSE.

ALSO, I TELL YOU THAT IF TWO OF
YOU ON EARTH AGREE ABOUT
SOMETHING, THEN YOU CAN PRAY
FOR IT. AND THE THING YOU ASK FOR
WILL BE DONE FOR YOU BY MY
FATHER IN HEAVEN. THIS IS TRUE
BECAUSE IF TWO OR THREE PEOPLE
COME TOGETHER IN MY NAME, I AM
THERE WITH THEM.
MATT. 18:19-20

S UMMARIZE IN YOUR OWN WORDS.
WHAT IS THIS BIBLE VERSE ABOUT?

T HINK ABOUT GOD'S ADVICE AND HIS PROMISE IN THIS VERSE.
WHAT IS HE TELLING YOU TO DO?

E XPLAIN HOW THIS BIBLE VERSE RELATES TO YOUR EXPERIENCES.
HOW CAN YOU USE THIS VERSE IN YOUR OWN LIFE?

P PRAY FOR GOD'S GUIDANCE AND HELP. WRITE A PRAYER LETTER
TO GOD. USE WORDS OR PHRASES FROM THE BIBLE VERSE.

THERE MIGHT BE A POOR MAN AMONG YOU. HE MIGHT BE IN ONE OF THE TOWNS OF THE LAND THE LORD YOUR GOD IS GIVING YOU. DO NOT BE SELFISH OR GREEDY TOWARD YOUR POOR BROTHER. BUT GIVE FREELY TO HIM. FREELY LEND HIM WHATEVER HE NEEDS.

DEUTERONOMY 15:7-8

S
UMMARIZE IN YOUR OWN WORDS.
WHAT IS THIS BIBLE VERSE ABOUT?

T
HINK ABOUT GOD'S ADVICE AND HIS PROMISE IN THIS VERSE.
WHAT IS HE TELLING YOU TO DO?

E
XPLAIN HOW THIS BIBLE VERSE RELATES TO YOUR EXPERIENCES.
HOW CAN YOU USE THIS VERSE IN YOUR OWN LIFE?

P
PRAY FOR GOD'S GUIDANCE AND HELP. WRITE A PRAYER LETTER
TO GOD. USE WORDS OR PHRASES FROM THE BIBLE VERSE.

BE STRONG AND BRAVE. DON'T BE AFRAID
OF THEM. DON'T BE FRIGHTENED. THE
LORD YOUR GOD WILL GO WITH YOU. HE
WILL NOT LEAVE YOU OR FORGET YOU.
DEUTERONOMY 31:6

S UMMARIZE IN YOUR OWN WORDS. WHAT IS THIS BIBLE VERSE ABOUT?

T HINK ABOUT GOD'S ADVICE AND HIS PROMISE IN THIS VERSE. WHAT IS HE TELLING YOU TO DO?

E XPLAIN HOW THIS BIBLE VERSE RELATES TO YOUR EXPERIENCES. HOW CAN YOU USE THIS VERSE IN YOUR OWN LIFE?

P PRAY FOR GOD'S GUIDANCE AND HELP. WRITE A PRAYER LETTER TO GOD. USE WORDS OR PHRASES FROM THE BIBLE VERSE.

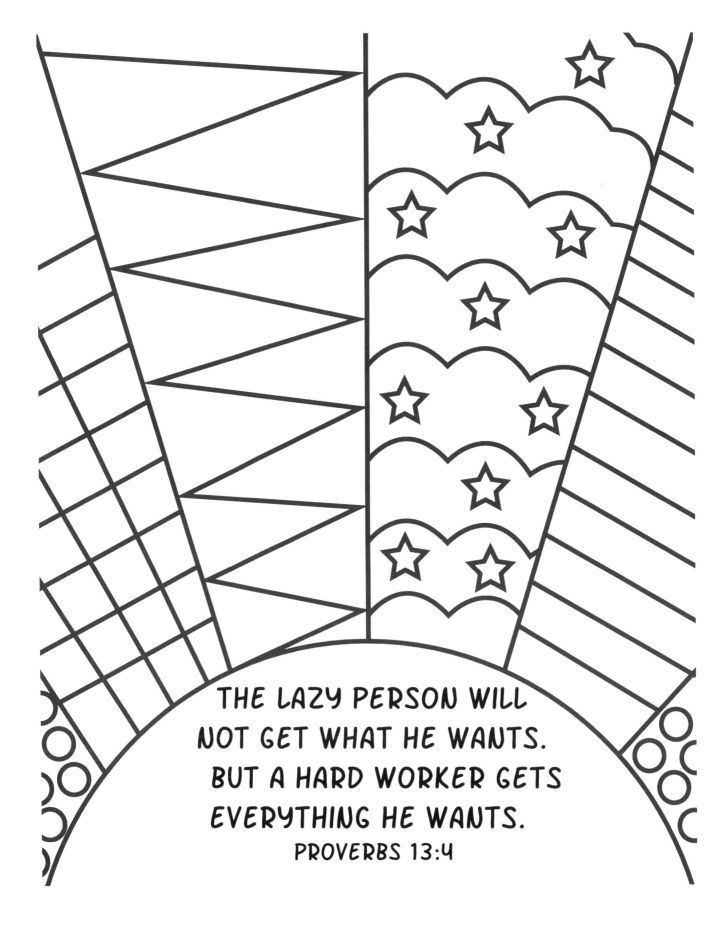

THE LAZY PERSON WILL
NOT GET WHAT HE WANTS.
BUT A HARD WORKER GETS
EVERYTHING HE WANTS.
PROVERBS 13:4

S UMMARIZE IN YOUR OWN WORDS. WHAT IS THIS BIBLE VERSE ABOUT?

T HINK ABOUT GOD'S ADVICE AND HIS PROMISE IN THIS VERSE. WHAT IS HE TELLING YOU TO DO?

E XPLAIN HOW THIS BIBLE VERSE RELATES TO YOUR EXPERIENCES. HOW CAN YOU USE THIS VERSE IN YOUR OWN LIFE?

P PRAY FOR GOD'S GUIDANCE AND HELP. WRITE A PRAYER LETTER TO GOD. USE WORDS OR PHRASES FROM THE BIBLE VERSE.

DO NOT LET THOSE EVIL PEOPLE LEAD YOU
AWAY BY THE WRONG THEY DO. BE CAREFUL SO
THAT YOU WILL NOT FALL FROM YOUR OWN
STRONG FAITH. BUT GROW IN THE GRACE AND
KNOWLEDGE OF OUR LORD AND SAVIOR JESUS
CHRIST.
2 PETER 3:17-18

S UMMARIZE IN YOUR OWN WORDS. WHAT IS THIS BIBLE VERSE ABOUT?

T HINK ABOUT GOD'S ADVICE AND HIS PROMISE IN THIS VERSE. WHAT IS HE TELLING YOU TO DO?

E XPLAIN HOW THIS BIBLE VERSE RELATES TO YOUR EXPERIENCES. HOW CAN YOU USE THIS VERSE IN YOUR OWN LIFE?

P PRAY FOR GOD'S GUIDANCE AND HELP. WRITE A PRAYER LETTER TO GOD. USE WORDS OR PHRASES FROM THE BIBLE VERSE.

GIVE, AND YOU WILL RECEIVE. YOU WILL BE GIVEN MUCH. IT WILL BE POURED INTO YOUR HANDS - MORE THAN YOU CAN HOLD. YOU WILL BE GIVEN SO MUCH THAT IT WILL SPILL INTO YOUR LAP. THE WAY YOU GIVE TO OTHERS IS THE WAY GOD WILL GIVE TO YOU.

LUKE 6:38

SUMMARIZE IN YOUR OWN WORDS.
WHAT IS THIS BIBLE VERSE ABOUT?

THINK ABOUT GOD'S ADVICE AND HIS PROMISE IN THIS VERSE.
WHAT IS HE TELLING YOU TO DO?

EXPLAIN HOW THIS BIBLE VERSE RELATES TO YOUR EXPERIENCES.
HOW CAN YOU USE THIS VERSE IN YOUR OWN LIFE?

PPRAY FOR GOD'S GUIDANCE AND HELP. WRITE A PRAYER LETTER
TO GOD. USE WORDS OR PHRASES FROM THE BIBLE VERSE.

DO NOT LIE TO EACH OTHER.
YOU HAVE LEFT YOUR OLD SINFUL
LIFE AND THE THINGS YOU DID BEFORE.
YOU HAVE BEGUN TO LIVE THE NEW LIFE.
IN YOUR NEW LIFE YOU ARE BEING MADE
NEW. YOU ARE BECOMING LIKE THE ONE WHO
MADE YOU. THIS NEW LIFE BRINGS YOU THE
TRUE KNOWLEDGE OF GOD.
COLOSSIANS 3:9-10

SUMMARIZE IN YOUR OWN WORDS. WHAT IS THIS BIBLE VERSE ABOUT?

THINK ABOUT GOD'S ADVICE AND HIS PROMISE IN THIS VERSE. WHAT IS HE TELLING YOU TO DO?

EXPLAIN HOW THIS BIBLE VERSE RELATES TO YOUR EXPERIENCES. HOW CAN YOU USE THIS VERSE IN YOUR OWN LIFE?

PRAY FOR GOD'S GUIDANCE AND HELP. WRITE A PRAYER LETTER TO GOD. USE WORDS OR PHRASES FROM THE BIBLE VERSE.

THEY WILL FIGHT AGAINST YOU.
BUT THEY WILL NOT DEFEAT YOU.
THIS IS BECAUSE I AM WITH
YOU, AND I WILL SAVE YOU!
SAYS THE LORD.
JEREMIAH 1:19

SUMMARIZE IN YOUR OWN WORDS. WHAT IS THIS BIBLE VERSE ABOUT?

THINK ABOUT GOD'S ADVICE AND HIS PROMISE IN THIS VERSE. WHAT IS HE TELLING YOU TO DO?

EXPLAIN HOW THIS BIBLE VERSE RELATES TO YOUR EXPERIENCES. HOW CAN YOU USE THIS VERSE IN YOUR OWN LIFE?

PRAY FOR GOD'S GUIDANCE AND HELP. WRITE A PRAYER LETTER TO GOD. USE WORDS OR PHRASES FROM THE BIBLE VERSE.

WE HAVE TROUBLES ALL AROUND US, BUT WE ARE NOT DEFEATED. WE DO NOT KNOW WHAT TO DO, BUT WE DO NOT GIVE UP. WE ARE PERSECUTED, BUT GOD DOES NOT LEAVE US. WE ARE HURT SOMETIMES, BUT WE ARE NOT DESTROYED. 2 CORINTHIANS 4:8-9

SUMMARIZE IN YOUR OWN WORDS.
WHAT IS THIS BIBLE VERSE ABOUT?

THINK ABOUT GOD'S ADVICE AND HIS PROMISE IN THIS VERSE.
WHAT IS HE TELLING YOU TO DO?

EXPLAIN HOW THIS BIBLE VERSE RELATES TO YOUR EXPERIENCES.
HOW CAN YOU USE THIS VERSE IN YOUR OWN LIFE?

PRAY FOR GOD'S GUIDANCE AND HELP. WRITE A PRAYER LETTER
TO GOD. USE WORDS OR PHRASES FROM THE BIBLE VERSE.

I CAN DO ALL THINGS THROUGH CHRIST BECAUSE HE GIVES ME STRENGTH. PHILIPPIANS 4:13

SUMMARIZE IN YOUR OWN WORDS.
WHAT IS THIS BIBLE VERSE ABOUT?

THINK ABOUT GOD'S ADVICE AND HIS PROMISE IN THIS VERSE.
WHAT IS HE TELLING YOU TO DO?

EXPLAIN HOW THIS BIBLE VERSE RELATES TO YOUR EXPERIENCES.
HOW CAN YOU USE THIS VERSE IN YOUR OWN LIFE?

PRAY FOR GOD'S GUIDANCE AND HELP. WRITE A PRAYER LETTER
TO GOD. USE WORDS OR PHRASES FROM THE BIBLE VERSE.

"DON'T SAY, 'I AM ONLY A BOY.' YOU MUST GO
EVERYWHERE THAT I SEND YOU. YOU MUST SAY
EVERYTHING I TELL YOU TO SAY. DON'T BE
AFRAID OF ANYONE, BECAUSE I AM WITH YOU.
I WILL PROTECT YOU," SAYS THE LORD.
JEREMIAH 1:6-8

S UMMARIZE IN YOUR OWN WORDS. WHAT IS THIS BIBLE VERSE ABOUT?

T HINK ABOUT GOD'S ADVICE AND HIS PROMISE IN THIS VERSE. WHAT IS HE TELLING YOU TO DO?

E XPLAIN HOW THIS BIBLE VERSE RELATES TO YOUR EXPERIENCES. HOW CAN YOU USE THIS VERSE IN YOUR OWN LIFE?

P PRAY FOR GOD'S GUIDANCE AND HELP. WRITE A PRAYER LETTER TO GOD. USE WORDS OR PHRASES FROM THE BIBLE VERSE.

I HAVE FOUGHT THE GOOD FIGHT. I HAVE FINISHED THE RACE. I HAVE KEPT THE FAITH. 2 TIMOTHY 4:7

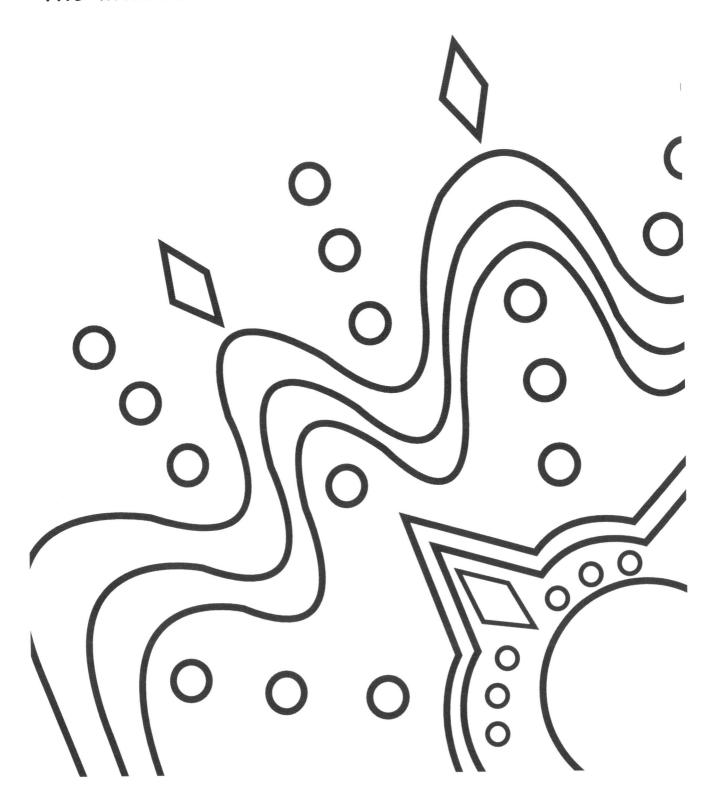

S UMMARIZE IN YOUR OWN WORDS. WHAT IS THIS BIBLE VERSE ABOUT?

T HINK ABOUT GOD'S ADVICE AND HIS PROMISE IN THIS VERSE. WHAT IS HE TELLING YOU TO DO?

E XPLAIN HOW THIS BIBLE VERSE RELATES TO YOUR EXPERIENCES. HOW CAN YOU USE THIS VERSE IN YOUR OWN LIFE?

P PRAY FOR GOD'S GUIDANCE AND HELP. WRITE A PRAYER LETTER TO GOD. USE WORDS OR PHRASES FROM THE BIBLE VERSE.

YOU ARE YOUNG, BUT DO NOT LET ANYONE TREAT YOU AS IF YOU WERE NOT IMPORTANT. BE AN EXAMPLE TO SHOW BELIEVERS HOW THEY SHOULD LIVE. SHOW THEM WITH YOUR WORDS,

WITH THE WAY THAT YOU LIVE, WITH YOUR LOVE, WITH YOUR FAITH, AND WITH YOUR PURE LIFE.
1 TIMOTHY 4:12

SUMMARIZE IN YOUR OWN WORDS.
WHAT IS THIS BIBLE VERSE ABOUT?

THINK ABOUT GOD'S ADVICE AND HIS PROMISE IN THIS VERSE.
WHAT IS HE TELLING YOU TO DO?

EXPLAIN HOW THIS BIBLE VERSE RELATES TO YOUR EXPERIENCES.
HOW CAN YOU USE THIS VERSE IN YOUR OWN LIFE?

PRAY FOR GOD'S GUIDANCE AND HELP. WRITE A PRAYER LETTER
TO GOD. USE WORDS OR PHRASES FROM THE BIBLE VERSE.

SUMMARIZE IN YOUR OWN WORDS. WHAT IS THIS BIBLE VERSE ABOUT?

THINK ABOUT GOD'S ADVICE AND HIS PROMISE IN THIS VERSE. WHAT IS HE TELLING YOU TO DO?

EXPLAIN HOW THIS BIBLE VERSE RELATES TO YOUR EXPERIENCES. HOW CAN YOU USE THIS VERSE IN YOUR OWN LIFE?

PRAY FOR GOD'S GUIDANCE AND HELP. WRITE A PRAYER LETTER TO GOD. USE WORDS OR PHRASES FROM THE BIBLE VERSE.

GOD DOES NOT SEE THE SAME WAY PEOPLE SEE.
PEOPLE LOOK AT THE OUTSIDE OF A PERSON, BUT
THE LORD LOOKS AT THE HEART.
SAMUEL 16:7

SUMMARIZE IN YOUR OWN WORDS.
WHAT IS THIS BIBLE VERSE ABOUT?

THINK ABOUT GOD'S ADVICE AND HIS PROMISE IN THIS VERSE.
WHAT IS HE TELLING YOU TO DO?

EXPLAIN HOW THIS BIBLE VERSE RELATES TO YOUR EXPERIENCES.
HOW CAN YOU USE THIS VERSE IN YOUR OWN LIFE?

PRAY FOR GOD'S GUIDANCE AND HELP. WRITE A PRAYER LETTER
TO GOD. USE WORDS OR PHRASES FROM THE BIBLE VERSE.

SO I ASK THAT YOU GIVE ME
WISDOM. THEN I CAN RULE THE
PEOPLE IN THE RIGHT WAY. THEN I WILL
KNOW THE DIFFERENCE BETWEEN RIGHT AND
WRONG. WITHOUT WISDOM, IT IS IMPOSSIBLE
TO RULE THIS GREAT PEOPLE OF YOURS.
1 KINGS 3:9

S UMMARIZE IN YOUR OWN WORDS. WHAT IS THIS BIBLE VERSE ABOUT?

T HINK ABOUT GOD'S ADVICE AND HIS PROMISE IN THIS VERSE. WHAT IS HE TELLING YOU TO DO?

E XPLAIN HOW THIS BIBLE VERSE RELATES TO YOUR EXPERIENCES. HOW CAN YOU USE THIS VERSE IN YOUR OWN LIFE?

P PRAY FOR GOD'S GUIDANCE AND HELP. WRITE A PRAYER LETTER TO GOD. USE WORDS OR PHRASES FROM THE BIBLE VERSE.

Page 74

YOU ARE MY SON AND I LOVE YOU.
I AM VERY PLEASED WITH YOU.

LUKE 3:22

S UMMARIZE IN YOUR OWN WORDS. WHAT IS THIS BIBLE VERSE ABOUT?

T HINK ABOUT GOD'S ADVICE AND HIS PROMISE IN THIS VERSE. WHAT IS HE TELLING YOU TO DO?

E XPLAIN HOW THIS BIBLE VERSE RELATES TO YOUR EXPERIENCES. HOW CAN YOU USE THIS VERSE IN YOUR OWN LIFE?

P PRAY FOR GOD'S GUIDANCE AND HELP. WRITE A PRAYER LETTER TO GOD. USE WORDS OR PHRASES FROM THE BIBLE VERSE.

HAVE COURAGE! IT IS I! DON'T BE AFRAID.
MATTHEW 14:27

S UMMARIZE IN YOUR OWN WORDS. WHAT IS THIS BIBLE VERSE ABOUT?

T HINK ABOUT GOD'S ADVICE AND HIS PROMISE IN THIS VERSE. WHAT IS HE TELLING YOU TO DO?

E XPLAIN HOW THIS BIBLE VERSE RELATES TO YOUR EXPERIENCES. HOW CAN YOU USE THIS VERSE IN YOUR OWN LIFE?

P PRAY FOR GOD'S GUIDANCE AND HELP. WRITE A PRAYER LETTER TO GOD. USE WORDS OR PHRASES FROM THE BIBLE VERSE.

SO DON'T WORRY, BECAUSE I AM WITH YOU. DON'T BE AFRAID, BECAUSE I AM YOUR GOD. I WILL MAKE YOU STRONG AND WILL HELP YOU. I WILL SUPPORT YOU WITH MY RIGHT HAND THAT SAVES YOU.
ISAIAH 41:10

SUMMARIZE IN YOUR OWN WORDS. WHAT IS THIS BIBLE VERSE ABOUT?

THINK ABOUT GOD'S ADVICE AND HIS PROMISE IN THIS VERSE. WHAT IS HE TELLING YOU TO DO?

EXPLAIN HOW THIS BIBLE VERSE RELATES TO YOUR EXPERIENCES. HOW CAN YOU USE THIS VERSE IN YOUR OWN LIFE?

PRAY FOR GOD'S GUIDANCE AND HELP. WRITE A PRAYER LETTER TO GOD. USE WORDS OR PHRASES FROM THE BIBLE VERSE.

S UMMARIZE IN YOUR OWN WORDS.
WHAT IS THIS BIBLE VERSE ABOUT?

T HINK ABOUT GOD'S ADVICE AND HIS PROMISE IN THIS VERSE.
WHAT IS HE TELLING YOU TO DO?

E XPLAIN HOW THIS BIBLE VERSE RELATES TO YOUR EXPERIENCES.
HOW CAN YOU USE THIS VERSE IN YOUR OWN LIFE?

P RAY FOR GOD'S GUIDANCE AND HELP. WRITE A PRAYER LETTER
TO GOD. USE WORDS OR PHRASES FROM THE BIBLE VERSE.

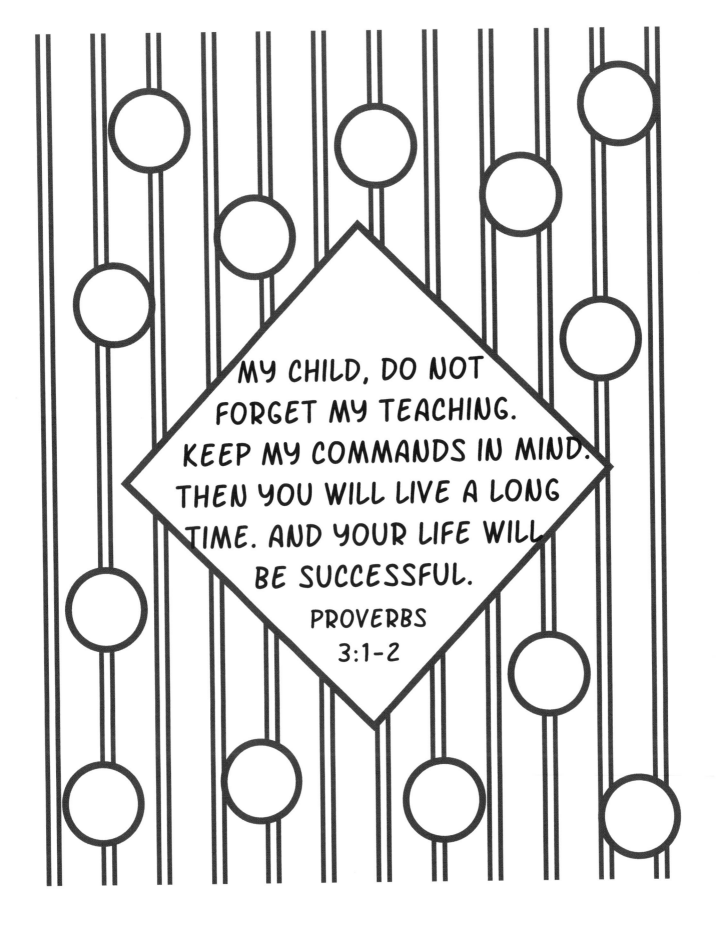

S UMMARIZE IN YOUR OWN WORDS. WHAT IS THIS BIBLE VERSE ABOUT?

T HINK ABOUT GOD'S ADVICE AND HIS PROMISE IN THIS VERSE. WHAT IS HE TELLING YOU TO DO?

E XPLAIN HOW THIS BIBLE VERSE RELATES TO YOUR EXPERIENCES. HOW CAN YOU USE THIS VERSE IN YOUR OWN LIFE?

P PRAY FOR GOD'S GUIDANCE AND HELP. WRITE A PRAYER LETTER TO GOD. USE WORDS OR PHRASES FROM THE BIBLE VERSE.

SOME PEOPLE PRETEND TO BE RICH BUT REALLY HAVE NOTHING. OTHER PEOPLE PRETEND TO BE POOR BUT REALLY ARE WEALTHY.

PROVERBS 13:7

S UMMARIZE IN YOUR OWN WORDS. WHAT IS THIS BIBLE VERSE ABOUT?

T HINK ABOUT GOD'S ADVICE AND HIS PROMISE IN THIS VERSE. WHAT IS HE TELLING YOU TO DO?

E XPLAIN HOW THIS BIBLE VERSE RELATES TO YOUR EXPERIENCES. HOW CAN YOU USE THIS VERSE IN YOUR OWN LIFE?

P PRAY FOR GOD'S GUIDANCE AND HELP. WRITE A PRAYER LETTER TO GOD. USE WORDS OR PHRASES FROM THE BIBLE VERSE.

WHOEVER SPENDS TIME WITH WISE
PEOPLE WILL BECOME WISE. BUT
WHOEVER MAKES FRIENDS WITH
FOOLS WILL SUFFER.
PROVERBS 13:20

SUMMARIZE IN YOUR OWN WORDS. WHAT IS THIS BIBLE VERSE ABOUT?

THINK ABOUT GOD'S ADVICE AND HIS PROMISE IN THIS VERSE. WHAT IS HE TELLING YOU TO DO?

EXPLAIN HOW THIS BIBLE VERSE RELATES TO YOUR EXPERIENCES. HOW CAN YOU USE THIS VERSE IN YOUR OWN LIFE?

PRAY FOR GOD'S GUIDANCE AND HELP. WRITE A PRAYER LETTER TO GOD. USE WORDS OR PHRASES FROM THE BIBLE VERSE.

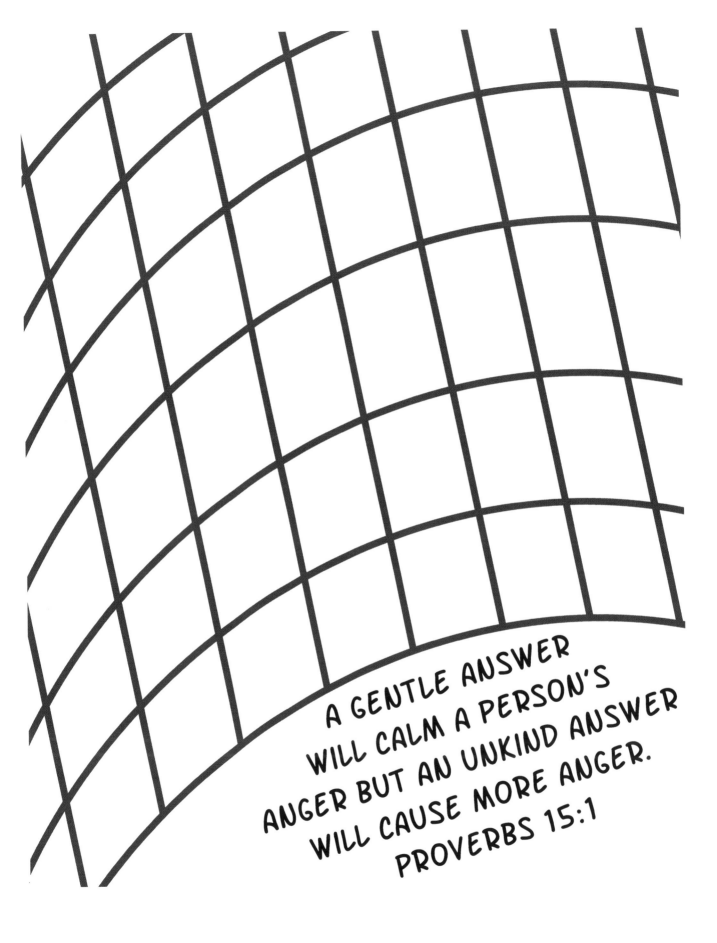

A GENTLE ANSWER
WILL CALM A PERSON'S
ANGER BUT AN UNKIND ANSWER
WILL CAUSE MORE ANGER.
PROVERBS 15:1

S UMMARIZE IN YOUR OWN WORDS. WHAT IS THIS BIBLE VERSE ABOUT?

T HINK ABOUT GOD'S ADVICE AND HIS PROMISE IN THIS VERSE. WHAT IS HE TELLING YOU TO DO?

E XPLAIN HOW THIS BIBLE VERSE RELATES TO YOUR EXPERIENCES. HOW CAN YOU USE THIS VERSE IN YOUR OWN LIFE?

P PRAY FOR GOD'S GUIDANCE AND HELP. WRITE A PRAYER LETTER TO GOD. USE WORDS OR PHRASES FROM THE BIBLE VERSE.

WE KNOW THAT IN EVERYTHING GOD WORKS FOR THE
GOOD OF THOSE WHO LOVE HIM. THEY ARE THE PEOPLE
GOD CALLED, BECAUSE THAT WAS HIS PLAN.
ROMANS 8:28

SUMMARIZE IN YOUR OWN WORDS. WHAT IS THIS BIBLE VERSE ABOUT?

THINK ABOUT GOD'S ADVICE AND HIS PROMISE IN THIS VERSE. WHAT IS HE TELLING YOU TO DO?

EXPLAIN HOW THIS BIBLE VERSE RELATES TO YOUR EXPERIENCES. HOW CAN YOU USE THIS VERSE IN YOUR OWN LIFE?

PRAY FOR GOD'S GUIDANCE AND HELP. WRITE A PRAYER LETTER TO GOD. USE WORDS OR PHRASES FROM THE BIBLE VERSE.

BUT THE SPIRIT GIVES LOVE, JOY, PEACE, PATIENCE, KINDNESS, GOODNESS, FAITHFULNESS, GENTLENESS, SELF-CONTROL. THERE IS NO LAW THAT SAYS THESE THINGS ARE WRONG.

GALATIANS 5:22-23

S UMMARIZE IN YOUR OWN WORDS. WHAT IS THIS BIBLE VERSE ABOUT?

T HINK ABOUT GOD'S ADVICE AND HIS PROMISE IN THIS VERSE. WHAT IS HE TELLING YOU TO DO?

E XPLAIN HOW THIS BIBLE VERSE RELATES TO YOUR EXPERIENCES. HOW CAN YOU USE THIS VERSE IN YOUR OWN LIFE?

P PRAY FOR GOD'S GUIDANCE AND HELP. WRITE A PRAYER LETTER TO GOD. USE WORDS OR PHRASES FROM THE BIBLE VERSE.

I HAVE GOOD PLANS FOR YOU. I DON'T PLAN TO HURT YOU.I PLAN TO GIVE YOU HOPE AND A GOOD FUTURE. JEREMIAH 29:11

S UMMARIZE IN YOUR OWN WORDS. WHAT IS THIS BIBLE VERSE ABOUT?

T HINK ABOUT GOD'S ADVICE AND HIS PROMISE IN THIS VERSE. WHAT IS HE TELLING YOU TO DO?

E XPLAIN HOW THIS BIBLE VERSE RELATES TO YOUR EXPERIENCES. HOW CAN YOU USE THIS VERSE IN YOUR OWN LIFE?

P PRAY FOR GOD'S GUIDANCE AND HELP. WRITE A PRAYER LETTER TO GOD. USE WORDS OR PHRASES FROM THE BIBLE VERSE.

DO FOR OTHER
PEOPLE WHAT YOU
WANT THEM TO DO
FOR YOU.
LUKE 6:31

S UMMARIZE IN YOUR OWN WORDS.
WHAT IS THIS BIBLE VERSE ABOUT?

T HINK ABOUT GOD'S ADVICE AND HIS PROMISE IN THIS VERSE.
WHAT IS HE TELLING YOU TO DO?

E XPLAIN HOW THIS BIBLE VERSE RELATES TO YOUR EXPERIENCES.
HOW CAN YOU USE THIS VERSE IN YOUR OWN LIFE?

P PRAY FOR GOD'S GUIDANCE AND HELP. WRITE A PRAYER LETTER
TO GOD. USE WORDS OR PHRASES FROM THE BIBLE VERSE.

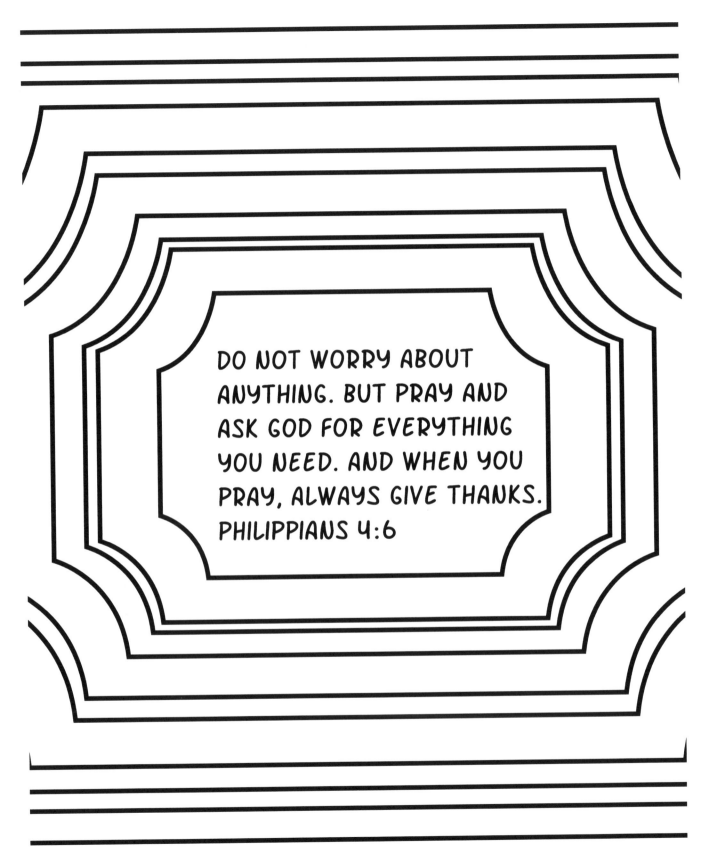

DO NOT WORRY ABOUT ANYTHING. BUT PRAY AND ASK GOD FOR EVERYTHING YOU NEED. AND WHEN YOU PRAY, ALWAYS GIVE THANKS. PHILIPPIANS 4:6

S UMMARIZE IN YOUR OWN WORDS.
WHAT IS THIS BIBLE VERSE ABOUT?

T HINK ABOUT GOD'S ADVICE AND HIS PROMISE IN THIS VERSE.
WHAT IS HE TELLING YOU TO DO?

E XPLAIN HOW THIS BIBLE VERSE RELATES TO YOUR EXPERIENCES.
HOW CAN YOU USE THIS VERSE IN YOUR OWN LIFE?

P PRAY FOR GOD'S GUIDANCE AND HELP. WRITE A PRAYER LETTER
TO GOD. USE WORDS OR PHRASES FROM THE BIBLE VERSE.

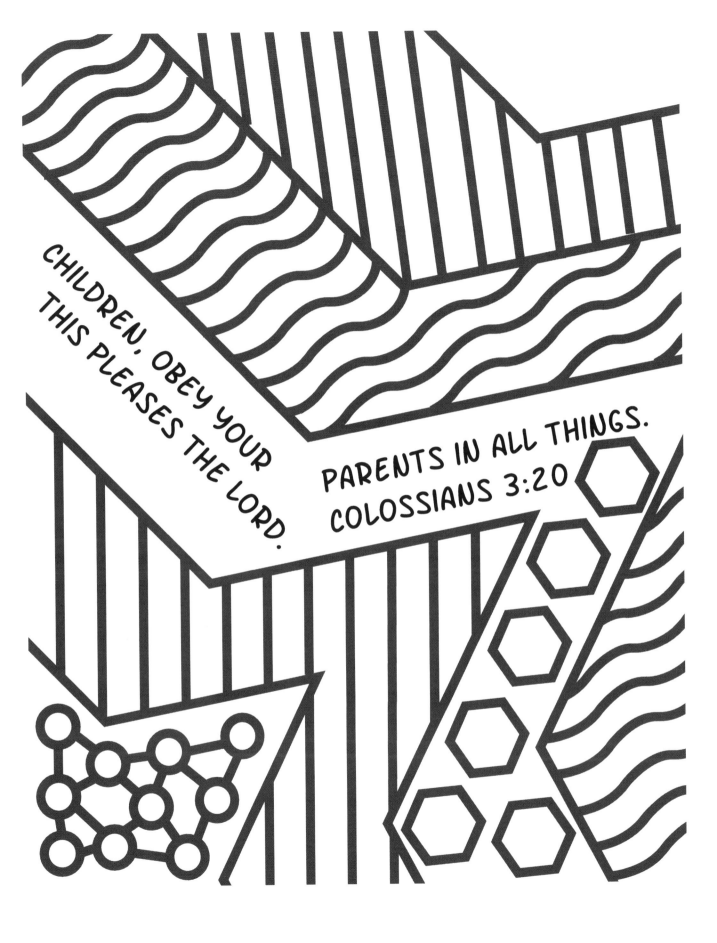

CHILDREN, OBEY YOUR THIS PLEASES THE LORD. PARENTS IN ALL THINGS. COLOSSIANS 3:20

S UMMARIZE IN YOUR OWN WORDS.
WHAT IS THIS BIBLE VERSE ABOUT?

T HINK ABOUT GOD'S ADVICE AND HIS PROMISE IN THIS VERSE.
WHAT IS HE TELLING YOU TO DO?

E XPLAIN HOW THIS BIBLE VERSE RELATES TO YOUR EXPERIENCES.
HOW CAN YOU USE THIS VERSE IN YOUR OWN LIFE?

P PRAY FOR GOD'S GUIDANCE AND HELP. WRITE A PRAYER LETTER
TO GOD. USE WORDS OR PHRASES FROM THE BIBLE VERSE.

OUR FATHER IN HEAVEN, WE PRAY THAT YOUR NAME WILL ALWAYS BE KEPT HOLY. WE PRAY THAT YOUR KINGDOM WILL COME. WE PRAY THAT WHAT YOU WANT WILL BE DONE, HERE ON EARTH AS IT IS IN HEAVEN. GIVE US THE FOOD WE NEED FOR EACH DAY. FORGIVE THE SINS WE HAVE DONE, JUST AS WE HAVE FORGIVEN THOSE WHO DID WRONG TO US. AND DO NOT CAUSE US TO BE TESTED; BUT SAVE US FROM THE EVIL ONE.

MATTHEW 6:9-13

S UMMARIZE IN YOUR OWN WORDS. WHAT IS THIS BIBLE VERSE ABOUT?

T HINK ABOUT GOD'S ADVICE AND HIS PROMISE IN THIS VERSE. WHAT IS HE TELLING YOU TO DO?

E XPLAIN HOW THIS BIBLE VERSE RELATES TO YOUR EXPERIENCES. HOW CAN YOU USE THIS VERSE IN YOUR OWN LIFE?

P PRAY FOR GOD'S GUIDANCE AND HELP. WRITE A PRAYER LETTER TO GOD. USE WORDS OR PHRASES FROM THE BIBLE VERSE.

Made in the USA
San Bernardino, CA
15 December 2017